WORDS THAT SHAPED AMERICA

THE MOST POWERFUL WORDS OF THE AMERICAN REVOLUTION

GIVE ME LIBERTY! OR GIVE ME DEATH.

BY JEREMY MORLOCK

Gareth Stevens PUBLISHING

Please visit our website, www.garethstevens.com. For a free color catalog of all our high-quality books, call toll free 1-800-542-2595 or fax 1-877-542-2596.

Library of Congress Cataloging-in-Publication Data

Names: Morlock, Jeremy, author.
Title: The most powerful words of the American Revolution / Jeremy Morlock.
Description: New York : Gareth Stevens Publishing, 2020. | Series: Words that shaped America | Includes index.
Identifiers: LCCN 2019026604 | ISBN 9781538248126 | ISBN 9781538248133 (library binding) | ISBN 9781538248119 (paperback) | ISBN 9781538248140 (ebook)
Subjects: LCSH: United States--History--Revolution, 1775-1783--Juvenile literature. | United States--History--Revolution, 1775-1783--Quotations.
Classification: LCC E208 .M865 2020 | DDC 973.3--dc23
LC record available at https://lccn.loc.gov/2019026604

First Edition

Published in 2020 by
Gareth Stevens Publishing
111 East 14th Street, Suite 349
New York, NY 10003

Designer: Sarah Liddell
Editor: Therese Shea

Photo credits: Cover, p. 1 (main) Fœ/Wikimedia Commons; cover, p. 1 (inset) SecretName101/Wikimedia Commons; ink smear used throughout Itsmesimon/Shutterstock.com; border used throughout igorrita/Shutterstock.com; background used throughout Lukasz Szwaj/Shutterstock.com; pp. 5, 7, 9, 21 photo courtesy of Library of Congress; p. 6 OgreBot/Wikimedia Commons; p. 10 BotMultiChill/Wikimedia Commons; p. 11 Fernandezmv/Wikimedia Commons; p. 13 Soerfm/Wikimedia Commons; p. 15 DcoetzeeBot/Wikimedia Commons; p. 17 ~riley/Wikimedia Commons; p. 18 Pateca/Wikimedia Commons; p. 19 Jan Arkesteijn/Wikimedia Commons; p. 23 (*Common Sense*) Niki K/Wikimedia Commons; p. 23 (Thomas Paine) EMStephens/Wikimedia Commons; p. 25 Scewing/Wikimedia Commons; p. 27 Historical/Contributor/Corbis Historical/Getty Images.

Printed in the United States of America

CPSIA compliance information: Batch #CW20GS: For further information contact Gareth Stevens, New York, New York at 1-800-542-2595.

CONTENTS

Words in the glossary appear in **bold** type the first time they are used in the text.

"TAXATION WITHOUT REPRESENTATION"

Powerful spoken and written words shaped the American Revolution. Stories and ideas changed the way people living in America saw themselves and their situation. At first, most British colonists thought of themselves as part of Great Britain. Over time, more colonists became unhappy with the British government. In speeches and newspapers, some stated they were treated unfairly.

One of the colonists' main complaints was that they had no say in the British government. Parliament made laws for Great Britain and the lands it controlled. Those laws included taxes on the colonists. Voters living in Great Britain elected people to represent them in Parliament. The colonists had no vote or voice in Parliament, however. "Taxation without representation is **tyranny**" became the cry of angry colonists as they moved closer to war.

JAMES OTIS JR.

Massachusetts lawyer, speaker, and author James Otis Jr. wrote convincingly against taxation without representation. Otis wrote a pamphlet, or small book, called *The Rights of the British Colonies Asserted and Proved*. He argued, "The colonists, black and white, born here, are free born British subjects, and entitled to all the essential civil rights of such." Otis was badly hurt during a fight with a British official in 1769. A brain injury troubled him for the rest of his life.

The Stamp Act of 1765 taxed certain paper items. American colonists protested and even attacked the homes and offices of officials.

BEHIND THE WORDS

The rights of British subjects developed through laws and traditions over many years. American colonists thought they deserved the same rights.

"BY UNITING WE STAND, BY DIVIDING WE FALL"

The British Parliament passed the Townshend Acts in 1767. These laws created new taxes on items shipped to the colonies. The money raised was supposed to support the British government, which needed funds because of its recent war with France in the colonies. Colonists saw the Townshend Acts as attacks on their freedom. People from different colonies agreed not to buy the taxed items. They cooperated to demonstrate their unhappiness to the government.

John Dickinson of Pennsylvania wrote a song about the importance of Americans working together to protect their rights. "The Liberty Song" includes these lines: "Then join hand in hand, brave Americans all, by uniting we stand, by dividing we fall." Newspapers published the lyrics, which were set to the tune of a British navy song.

JOHN DICKINSON

BEHIND THE WORDS

WHEN JOHN DICKINSON WROTE "THE LIBERTY SONG" IN 1768, HE WASN'T CALLING FOR A REVOLUTION. IN FACT, THE LAST PART OF THE SONG WISHED GOOD HEALTH FOR THE KING AND WEALTH FOR GREAT BRITAIN.

BENJAMIN FRANKLIN PUBLISHED THIS CARTOON IN 1754, ENCOURAGING COOPERATION AMONG THE COLONIES DURING THE FRENCH AND INDIAN WAR. THE IMAGE WAS REUSED TO UNITE AMERICAN COLONISTS AGAINST THE BRITISH.

JOHN DICKINSON: PENMAN OF THE REVOLUTION

Lawyer, writer, and politician John Dickinson wrote "Letters from a Farmer in Pennsylvania," declaring the Townshend Acts were illegal because only the colonial governments could raise money. Dickinson represented Pennsylvania in the **Continental Congress** from 1774 to 1776. He refused to sign the Declaration of Independence, believing it was too early for such a strong action. However, he's still sometimes called the "Penman of the Revolution" because his writings inspired many to take up the cause of independence.

"GIVE ME LIBERTY, OR GIVE ME DEATH"

Patrick Henry was a Virginia leader and lawyer known for his powerful speeches. In 1765, he spoke out angrily about the Stamp Act. His words then were so strong that some accused him of treason.

By March 1775, Henry thought that Virginians should be prepared for a fight. He asked other Virginia patriot leaders to create a **militia**, training people and giving them weapons. Some Virginians still hoped for peace with Great Britain. But in a speech, Henry said it was too late—war had already started. Historians aren't sure of his exact words, but they're often said to have been: "I know not what course others may take; but as for me, give me liberty, or give me death!" Freedom was more important than danger to this patriot.

BEHIND THE WORDS

ONE OF THE VIRGINIA FIGHTING GROUPS FORMED WAS THE CULPEPPER MINUTEMEN. THEY CARRIED A FLAG WITH A PICTURE OF A RATTLESNAKE AND THE PHRASES "LIBERTY OR DEATH" AND "DON'T TREAD ON ME."

THE SECOND VIRGINIA CONVENTION

In 1774, the royal governor told Virginia's elected representatives not to meet. Virginia's patriot leaders gathered anyway. They first met in Williamsburg, the colony's capital. They worried the governor would stop them if they met there again. The next convention, or meeting, was in Richmond, Virginia. The Second Virginia Convention decided to create a fighting force and asked Patrick Henry, George Washington, Thomas Jefferson, and others to lead the effort.

THIS ILLUSTRATION CELEBRATES PATRICK HENRY'S SPEECH TO THE SECOND VIRGINIA CONVENTION. IT WAS PRINTED IN 1876, WHEN THE UNITED STATES WAS MARKING 100 YEARS OF INDEPENDENCE.

"LAWLESS COMMITTEEMEN"

Not all colonists wanted to separate from Great Britain. Loyalists, also called Tories, thought that they should obey Parliament and the king. Reverend Samuel Seabury believed the patriots were **exaggerating** the problems with Great Britain. As patriots created committees to address complaints against the British, Seabury viewed them as breaking the law. He was more afraid of his neighbors creating their own laws than the royal government, he said.

SAMUEL SEABURY

"If I must be enslaved let it be by a king at least, and not by a parcel of **upstart** lawless Committeemen," Seabury wrote. "If I must be devoured, let me be devoured by the jaws of a lion and not gnawed to death by rats and vermin." Seabury stated that the patriots' committees didn't represent all Americans.

RELIGION AND THE REVOLUTION

Religious leaders influenced thoughts on the American Revolution. The British king led the Church of England, so many of its ministers saw loyalty to Britain as a duty. Loyalist Samuel Seabury was a priest in the Church of England. Quaker teachings opposed violence, while Congregational minister Jonathan Mayhew thought it was the "glorious" duty of Christians to fight tyranny. Some American churches separated from the churches of Europe after the war. For example, in America, the Church of England became the Episcopal Church.

SAMUEL SEABURY HAD REASONS TO FEAR LAWLESSNESS. IN JANUARY 1774, PATRIOTS ATTACKED A LOYALIST OFFICIAL NAMED JOHN MALCOM. THEY COVERED HIM IN HOT TAR AND FEATHERS.

BEHIND THE WORDS

PATRIOTS SET UP COMMITTEES OF CORRESPONDENCE IN DIFFERENT COLONIES TO SHARE INFORMATION WITH ONE ANOTHER AND WITH COLONISTS. THESE COMMITTEES LATER HELPED UNITE THE COLONIES IN WAR.

"THE WHITES OF THEIR EYES"

British soldiers and American militias faced each other in the Massachusetts towns of Lexington and Concord on April 19, 1775. These weren't large battles, though. The first major battle took place near Boston on June 17, 1775.

During this conflict, the Battle of Bunker Hill, Colonel William Prescott led the colonists, who built defenses at the top of a hill near Boston. American officers ordered their men not to shoot until the British were very close. Stories say one of the militia officers instructed: "Don't fire until you see the whites of their eyes." This way, the Americans could save **ammunition** and do the most harm to the enemy. The British won the battle but lost many soldiers. The Americans had shown they wouldn't give up easily.

BEHIND THE WORDS

HISTORIANS AREN'T SURE IF "DON'T FIRE UNTIL YOU SEE THE WHITES OF THEIR EYES" WERE THE EXACT WORDS SAID AT THE BATTLE. IT'S NOT CLEAR WHO GAVE THAT ORDER EITHER.

The artist John Trumbull witnessed the Battle of Bunker Hill. Years later, he created this painting to remember the death of Joseph Warren.

Joseph Warren: War Hero

Americans lost some early battles but spread stories about the bravery of their fighters and the justness of their cause. These tales pushed more people to support the patriots. Joseph Warren was a Massachusetts doctor and patriot leader whose deeds had given him a reputation as a bold revolutionary. For example, he sent Paul Revere to warn Lexington and Concord that the British planned to seize ammunition and weapons. Warren was killed at the Battle of Bunker Hill.

"THE UNHAPPY AND DELUDED MULTITUDE"

British leaders didn't want to give up control of the colonies. They hoped that strong and quick action would change the minds of the colonists. King George III told Parliament in October 1775 that military force would discourage colonists pushing for independence and encourage loyalists. "When the unhappy and **deluded** multitude, against whom this force will be directed, shall become sensible of their error, I shall be ready to receive the misled with tenderness and mercy," King George said.

The king believed that lies and exaggerations had fooled many colonists, but British military power would force them into obedience. King George asked Parliament to approve plans for the British navy and army to transport ships and soldiers to America. Parliament voted for this military action.

BEHIND THE WORDS

GREAT BRITAIN RULED COLONIES IN MANY PARTS OF THE WORLD AND HAD A STRONG ARMY AND NAVY. THE AMERICAN COLONIES AND THEIR RESOURCES WERE VIEWED AS TOO VALUABLE TO LOSE.

PARLIAMENT AND THE KING

George III was the British king, but he didn't rule alone. Parliament controlled spending and created laws. Over hundreds of years, Parliament had forced past kings to give up more and more control. During the 17th century, Parliament and King Charles I had a power struggle. Finally, Parliament ordered Charles I to be executed. Even though the monarchy was restored 11 years later, Parliament had secured the rights of the people against the power of a ruler.

This painting of George III from the 1760s displays the king's wealth and power.

"ALL MEN ARE CREATED EQUAL"

The Second Continental Congress voted in 1776 to break away from Great Britain. Patriot leaders wanted to convince the world they had good reason. They focused on the idea of natural rights, or those rights people are born with, that should not be taken away. The Congress approved the Declaration of Independence, which states: "We hold these truths to be self-evident, that all men are created equal, that they are endowed [provided] by their Creator with certain **unalienable** Rights, that among these are Life, Liberty and the pursuit of Happiness."

Power should come from the people, not the government, according to the patriots. The Declaration of Independence stated the British government had ignored the people's rights and harmed the colonies. The American people needed to create a government to protect individual freedom.

ALL MEN?

The Continental Congress talked of natural rights, but only considered the rights of some people. British law mostly protected the rights of men who owned land. The new American government followed similar ways of thinking. Women, people in slavery, and Native Americans weren't given the same protections. Thomas Jefferson, the main author of the Declaration of Independence, kept slaves while writing about freedom. He called slavery evil, but didn't see an end to it.

THOMAS JEFFERSON WROTE MOST OF THE DECLARATION OF INDEPENDENCE. BENJAMIN FRANKLIN, JOHN ADAMS, AND OTHERS HELPED PREPARE IT FOR THE SECOND CONTINENTAL CONGRESS TO APPROVE.

BEHIND THE WORDS

THE BEGINNING OF THE DECLARATION OF INDEPENDENCE IS SIMILAR TO THE EARLIER VIRGINIA DECLARATION OF RIGHTS. THE VIRGINIA DECLARATION CLAIMS RIGHTS TO "THE ENJOYMENT OF LIFE AND LIBERTY, WITH THE MEANS OF ACQUIRING AND POSSESSING PROPERTY, AND PURSUING AND OBTAINING HAPPINESS AND SAFETY."

"REMEMBER THE LADIES"

The Continental Congress first worked to speak for the colonies, then to create a new American government. All the delegates were white men, however. Abigail Adams wrote to her husband, John Adams, who was representing Massachusetts: "I desire you would remember the ladies, and be more generous and favourable to them than your ancestors. Do not put such unlimited power into the hands of the husbands. Remember all men would be tyrants if they could."

Abigail wished a new kind of government would form, one that would consider the well-being of women when making laws. She didn't suggest that women should vote but did worry that their needs would be ignored, noting that they had no voice or representation in Congress. However, it was many years until American women enjoyed similar rights to men.

ABIGAIL ADAMS

MERCY OTIS WARREN

Abigail Adams was a friend of another powerful female voice of the American Revolution: Mercy Otis Warren. Like Adams, Warren, who was the sister of James Otis Jr., believed that women were unfairly excluded from opportunities that men enjoyed. She was heavily involved in the war, writing plays that reflected her thoughts about Great Britain and urging others to stand up for the rights of the colonies. "America stands armed with resolution and virtue," she said.

ABIGAIL ADAMS PRAISED MERCY OTIS WARREN'S PLAYS AGAINST GREAT BRITAIN AND ENCOURAGED HER TO KEEP WRITING.

BEHIND THE WORDS

ABIGAIL ADAMS BECAME THE FIRST LADY OF THE UNITED STATES WHEN HER HUSBAND JOHN ADAMS TOOK OFFICE AS PRESIDENT IN 1797. THEIR SON JOHN QUINCY ADAMS BECAME PRESIDENT IN 1825.

"ONE LIFE TO LOSE"

Nathan Hale was a teacher who joined a Connecticut militia near the start of the American Revolution. He fought near Boston, then headed to New York. There, he **volunteered** to spy on British forces. He had to travel into New York City, which was under British control, and report back about the positions and movements of British soldiers.

The British caught Hale in September 1776 and discovered his mission. They prepared to hang him. According to American folklore, Hale was calm and brave even though he knew that he was about to die. He spoke about his love for his new nation. His last words were said to be: "I only regret that I have but one life to lose for my country." Hale's willingness to sacrifice himself inspired other Americans.

BEHIND THE WORDS

ARMIES DURING THAT TIME WERE EXPECTED TO KEEP CAPTURED SOLDIERS AS PRISONERS. SPIES WERE TREATED DIFFERENTLY AND KILLED. HALE KNEW THE DANGER HE FACED.

Nathan Hale was executed as a spy, but his reputation and fame grew. This illustration displaying Hale's bravery was created more than 80 years after his death.

AMERICAN SPIES

Patriot spies came from many backgrounds. Anna Strong had a farm on Long Island. She hung clothes on a line in a certain way to send coded messages to patriots. Robert Townsend was a patriot who pretended to be a loyalist in order to gain British trust—and information. James Armistead Lafayette, a slave who volunteered with the American army, spied on the British, going to their army camps and pretending he had escaped from slavery.

"THE TIMES THAT TRY MEN'S SOULS"

Author Thomas Paine was talented at explaining the ideas behind the American Revolution. His words had urged people to push for independence. Paine felt the need to write again as the fighting continued. In his series of pamphlets *The American Crisis*, Paine said that war would be difficult. He called for the American people to keep fighting.

"These are the times that try men's souls," Paine wrote. "The summer soldier and the sunshine patriot will, in this crisis, shrink from the service of their country; but he that stands by it now, deserves the love and thanks of man and woman." Paine knew that people would get tired of the hardships of war. The true patriots, he said, were those who kept fighting.

BEHIND THE WORDS

GEORGE WASHINGTON THOUGHT THAT *THE AMERICAN CRISIS* WAS SO IMPORTANT THAT HE HAD OFFICERS READ IT TO HIS SOLDIERS BEFORE THEIR FAMOUS CROSSING OF THE DELAWARE RIVER IN DECEMBER 1776.

AFTER THE END OF THE AMERICAN REVOLUTION, THOMAS PAINE WENT ON TO BECOME INVOLVED IN THE **FRENCH REVOLUTION**.

COMMON SENSE;
ADDRESSED TO THE
INHABITANTS
OF
AMERICA,
On the following interesting
SUBJECTS.

I. Of the Origin and Design of Government in general, with concise Remarks on the English Constitution.

II. Of Monarchy and Hereditary Succession.

III. Thoughts on the present State of American Affairs.

IV. Of the present Ability of America, with some miscellaneous Reflections.

Man knows no Master save creating HEAVEN,
Or those whom choice and common good ordain.
THOMSON.

PHILADELPHIA;
Printed, and Sold, by R. BELL, in Third-Street.
MDCCLXXVI.

PAINE'S *COMMON SENSE*

Thomas Paine spent his early life in Great Britain. He moved to Pennsylvania in 1774 and became an important voice for independence. Paine wrote a pamphlet called *Common Sense* in early 1776. He argued against a monarch as head of government and said a continued connection with Britain would only limit America. An estimated 50,000 copies of *Common Sense* helped convince many that the colonies needed to be independent.

"GREAT TROUBLE TO ALL OUR NATIONS"

The American Revolution brought new difficulties to Native Americans. They had faced violence and lost land as the colonies grew. As the war continued, many couldn't avoid becoming involved.

"The disturbances in America give great trouble to all our Nations," Mohawk leader Thayendanegea, also called Joseph Brant, wrote to the British government. The Mohawk sided with the British, but Thayendanegea mentioned that the British hadn't kept past promises. "The Indians think it very hard they should have been so deceived by the white people," he wrote.

The Oneida people, however, sided with the Americans. They, too, suffered during the war. In 1783, Oneida leaders requested help and supplies from George Washington, asking, "Is this the fulfillment of all your fair promises that, at the last, we must die with hunger and cold?"

INTERNATIONAL RELATIONS

The British and the Americans each tried to get native peoples to join their side. Both looked for outside help as well. Americans hoped to get aid from France, which often clashed with Great Britain. At first, France helped through money and trade, but then sent soldiers and arms. Spain began a war with Great Britain. The Netherlands gave Americans loans to fund the war and also declared war on the British.

Thayendanegea traveled to Great Britain and met King George III near the start of the war.

BEHIND THE WORDS

The Mohawk had been part of the Haudenosaunee, or Iroquois Confederacy, for many years. So had the Oneida. The war divided the friendly nations.

"I HAVE NOT YET BEGUN TO FIGHT"

Some military leaders of the American Revolution stood out for their bravery. John Paul Jones, a captain in the new American navy, was one such inspiring leader.

On September 23, 1779, the American ship *Bonhomme Richard* battled the British ship *Serapis* near the coast of England. The American vessel was badly damaged early on. Soon, it was on fire and sinking. Yet, Captain John Paul Jones kept his sailors battling on. When the *Bonhomme Richard* lost its mast, its flag fell. The British captain yelled to Jones, asking if that meant they were surrendering. Jones wasn't ready to give up. He is said to have declared, "I have not yet begun to fight!" The Americans began firing again and finally forced the *Serapis* to surrender.

BEHIND THE WORDS

THE AMERICANS WANTED TO DISRUPT BRITISH TRADE AS A WAY OF FIGHTING THE WAR. THEY SENT JOHN PAUL JONES AND OTHERS TO ATTACK AND CAPTURE BRITISH MERCHANT SHIPS.

THE BATTLE OF THE *BONHOMME RICHARD* AND THE *SERAPIS* WAS FIERCE. IT WAS THE FIRST TIME AN AMERICAN SHIP DEFEATED A BRITISH SHIP IN BRITISH WATERS. THE *BONHOMME RICHARD* SANK THE NEXT DAY.

A FRENCH GIFT

The *Bonhomme Richard* had been a French merchant ship called the *Duc de Duras*. In 1779, the king of France gave it to the Americans. Captain John Paul Jones ordered that guns be added to it. He renamed the ship in honor of Benjamin Franklin, the first American **ambassador** to France. Franklin was also the author of *Poor Richard's Almanac*, published in France as *Les Maximes du Bonhomme Richard*.

"THE APPROACH OF A BRIGHTER DAY"

The support of France helped the United States wear down the British. The Siege of Yorktown, in Virginia, was the beginning of the end. American and French soldiers on land and French ships at sea surrounded the army of General Charles Cornwallis in the fall of 1781. Cut off from help and supplies, Cornwallis was forced to surrender.

BEHIND THE WORDS

EIGHT YEARS PASSED BETWEEN THE BATTLES AT LEXINGTON AND CONCORD AND THE OFFICIAL AGREEMENT TO STOP FIGHTING.

After years of deadly battles, the Americans and British agreed officially to stop all fighting in April 1783. General George Washington told his troops that the end of fighting "promises the approach of a brighter day, than hath hitherto [until now] illuminated the Western Hemisphere." Americans had won independence and protected their rights. Through hardship, suffering, and danger, they earned a better future.

THE MINDS OF THE PEOPLE

John Adams said the changes in Americans' ideas and opinions were more important than the fighting. He wrote in a letter to Thomas Jefferson, "The Revolution was in the minds of the people, and this was effected, from 1760 to 1775, in the course of fifteen years before a drop of blood was drawn at Lexington."

TIMELINE OF THE AMERICAN REVOLUTION

1764: JAMES OTIS PUBLISHES *THE RIGHTS OF THE BRITISH COLONIES ASSERTED AND PROVED.*

1766: AFTER PROTESTS, PARLIAMENT REPEALS THE STAMP ACT OF 1765.

1767: PARLIAMENT PASSES NEW TAXES CALLED THE TOWNSHEND ACTS.

1768: "THE LIBERTY SONG" BY JOHN DICKINSON IS PUBLISHED.

MARCH 1775: PATRICK HENRY GIVES HIS "LIBERTY OR DEATH" SPEECH.

APRIL 1775: THE BATTLES OF LEXINGTON AND CONCORD ARE FOUGHT.

JANUARY 1776: THOMAS PAINE PUBLISHES *COMMON SENSE.*

JULY 1776: THE DECLARATION OF INDEPENDENCE IS ADOPTED.

SEPTEMBER 1776: THE BRITISH EXECUTE AMERICAN NATHAN HALE.

DECEMBER 1776: THOMAS PAINE PUBLISHES THE FIRST PART OF *THE AMERICAN CRISIS.*

1779: THE *BONHOMME RICHARD* BATTLES THE *SERAPIS.*

1781: GENERAL CORNWALLIS SURRENDERS AT YORKTOWN.

1783: THE AMERICANS AND THE BRITISH SIGN THE TREATY OF PARIS, ENDING THE WAR.

GLOSSARY

ambassador: someone sent by one group or country to speak for it in different places

ammunition: bullets, shells, and other things fired by weapons

Continental Congress: a meeting of colonial representatives before, during, and after the American Revolution

deluded: believing something that is not true

exaggerate: to think of or describe something as larger or greater than it really is

French Revolution: a period of time in France when the people overthrew the monarchy and took control of the government, 1789 to 1799

militia: a group of citizens who organize like soldiers in order to protect themselves

tyranny: cruel and unfair treatment of others by people with power

unalienable: not capable of being taken away

upstart: describing successful people who are disrespectful to older and more experienced people

volunteer: to offer service without being asked

FOR MORE INFORMATION

BOOKS

Machajewski, Sarah. *Declaration of Independence.* New York, NY: PowerKids Press, 2016.

Murray, Stuart. *American Revolution.* New York, NY: DK Publishing, 2015.

WEBSITES

Continental Congress
www.history.com/topics/american-revolution/the-continental-congress
Learn about the work and changing role of the Continental Congress.

Creating the United States
www.loc.gov/exhibits/creating-the-united-states/revolution-of-the-mind.html
The Library of Congress explores the ideas that helped lead to the American Revolution.

The Declaration of Independence: A History
www.archives.gov/founding-docs/declaration-history
The National Archives tracks the steps that led to the signing of the Declaration of Independence.

INDEX